Original title:
Joyful Life

Author: Thor Castlebury
ISBN HARDBACK: 978-9916-88-146-0
ISBN PAPERBACK: 978-9916-88-147-7

Playful Shadows on the Wall

Beneath the moon's soft glow, they dance,
A ballet of light in fleeting chance.
Whispers of dusk in colors so bright,
Creating a tapestry of night.

Lullabies of Laughter

Echoes of joy in the gentle breeze,
Tickling the hearts, putting minds at ease.
Melodies weave through the starry skies,
As giggles and smiles begin to rise.

Savoring the Present

Moments like petals, delicate and sweet,
Holding them close, feeling life's heartbeat.
Time lingers softly, a tender embrace,
In the warmth of now, we find our place.

Raindrops of Contentment

Pattering softly on the windowsill,
Nature's own song, a comforting thrill.
Each drop a promise, a gift from above,
Filling our hearts with a tranquil love.

Embracing the Warmth of Today

The sun rises bright in the sky,
Warming the earth and spirit nearby.
Embracing each moment, so clear,
A chance to live fully, my dear.

With laughter and joy in the air,
We gather together, love to share.
Life's tender whispers, a gentle breeze,
Embracing our hearts with sweet ease.

Radiance in Each Heartbeat

Every heartbeat echoes with light,
Guiding our paths through the night.
In each breath, a story unfolds,
A tapestry of dreams, brave and bold.

With every step, we dance and sway,
Radiance blooming along the way.
Together we shine, a vibrant art,
As love captures the beat of the heart.

Savoring Sweet Fleeting Moments

Time slips like sand through our hands,
Yet in its wake, beauty expands.
We cling to the laughter, the smiles,
Savoring moments, cherished miles.

In whispers of joy, we find our song,
Sweet memories linger, where we belong.
With each fleeting second, we weave,
A tapestry of love, we believe.

Raindrops of Contentment

Pattering softly on the windowsill,
Nature's own song, a comforting thrill.
Each drop a promise, a gift from above,
Filling our hearts with a tranquil love.

Embracing the Warmth of Today

The sun rises bright in the sky,
Warming the earth and spirit nearby.
Embracing each moment, so clear,
A chance to live fully, my dear.

With laughter and joy in the air,
We gather together, love to share.
Life's tender whispers, a gentle breeze,
Embracing our hearts with sweet ease.

Radiance in Each Heartbeat

Every heartbeat echoes with light,
Guiding our paths through the night.
In each breath, a story unfolds,
A tapestry of dreams, brave and bold.

With every step, we dance and sway,
Radiance blooming along the way.
Together we shine, a vibrant art,
As love captures the beat of the heart.

Savoring Sweet Fleeting Moments

Time slips like sand through our hands,
Yet in its wake, beauty expands.
We cling to the laughter, the smiles,
Savoring moments, cherished miles.

In whispers of joy, we find our song,
Sweet memories linger, where we belong.
With each fleeting second, we weave,
A tapestry of love, we believe.

The Melody of Happiness Unfolding

Happiness hums in the air we breathe,
A melody twisting, winding, we weave.
With every note, joy takes its flight,
Unfolding the magic within our sight.

Together we dance to the rhythm of love,
Creating a symphony sent from above.
Each heartbeat in time, a chorus so grand,
Melodies of happiness, hand in hand.

A Quiet Serenade of Happiness

In soft whispers, joy takes flight,
Where laughter dances, warm and bright.
A gentle breeze, a tender sigh,
Filling our hearts, as moments fly.

Sunlight spills on paths we tread,
Painting dreams in shades of red.
With every step, our spirits soar,
In this symphony, we crave for more.

Flickers of Delight

In fleeting moments, sparks ignite,
A child's giggle, pure delight.
The twinkling stars, a whispered glow,
Guide us to where our joys can grow.

A spark of laughter, a gentle tease,
In shared stories, our hearts find ease.
With every tick of fleeting time,
These flickers of joy, a constant rhyme.

The Heart's Secret Playground

In shadows deep, where dreams ignite,
A playground where the heart takes flight.
Swinging high on hopes' embrace,
Finding solace in this hidden space.

With laughter echoing through the air,
Embracing joys, without a care.
In the heart's recesses, we shall play,
Forever young, come what may.

Notes of Triumph

In every struggle, courage blooms,
Resilience rises, breaking glooms.
Each note we play, a story told,
Of battles fought and hearts of gold.

With every triumph, we grow strong,
In the symphony where we belong.
Let the world hear our heartfelt song,
For in our spirits, courage throngs.

A Symphony of Grateful Hearts

In every note, a whisper sings,
Of life bestowed and simple things.
A harmony of joy we weave,
With thankful hearts, we truly believe.

Each beat resounds, a perfect rhyme,
In moments shared, we grasp our time.
Together we dance, our spirits soar,
In this grand symphony, forevermore.

Brimming with Light

Sunrise spills across the land,
Painting gold with gentle hand.
We chase the shadows, seek the bright,
Together we bask in radiant light.

Each smile we share reflects the day,
A beacon bright along the way.
With hearts aglow, we break the night,
In every moment, we're bathed in light.

The Art of Cherished Days

Brushstrokes of laughter fill the air,
In every moment, love is rare.
We capture time in colors bold,
The stories whispered, lovingly told.

Each fleeting hour, a masterpiece,
In every sigh, a sweet release.
With memories framed, we find our way,
In the art of cherished days.

Garden of Glee

In a garden where laughter grows,
Beneath the sun, the joy flows.
Each petal bright, each leaf a cheer,
In this haven, all is clear.

We plant our dreams with tender care,
Watered with love, a bond we share.
In every bloom, our spirits free,
We dance together, in the garden of glee.

Trails of Laughter

In the woods where laughter plays,
Friends and joy weave through the days.
Every step a spark of cheer,
Echoes of love ring crystal clear.

Through the trees the sunlight beams,
Chasing shadows, chasing dreams.
With every giggle, hearts unite,
In trails of laughter, pure delight.

Celebration of the Now

Gather here, beneath the skies,
Let our spirits rise and fly.
In this moment, let us share,
A celebration, free of care.

Savor flavors, smiles, and sights,
Every heartbeat, ignites the nights.
Together in this precious hour,
A bloom of joy, a blooming flower.

Navigating Waves of Exhilaration

On the ocean's vibrant crest,
Sailing forth, we feel our best.
Each wave dances, swift and bright,
Guiding dreams into the light.

Riding currents, spirits soar,
Navigating, we explore.
With every splash, the heart takes flight,
In waves of thrill, all feels right.

The Radiant Path Ahead

In the dawn's soft golden hue,
We find visions, bright and true.
Every step a chance to grow,
A radiant path, we will follow.

With courage in our open hearts,
Embracing change as life imparts.
The future glows, a vibrant thread,
Together on the path ahead.

The Radiance of Togetherness

In the glow of shared dreams,
We find warmth in each smile,
Hands entwined in moments,
Together, we walk each mile.

Underneath the starlit skies,
Whispers dance in the night,
In laughter we build our lives,
With hearts full of pure light.

Time wraps us in its arms,
As we celebrate each day,
In the bond of our love,
We never lose our way.

With every breath we take,
A promise etched in time,
United, we create,
A harmony so sublime.

Bubbles of Delight in the Air

Floating softly through the sky,
Bubbles glimmer, full of cheer,
Each a wish that drifts on by,
Carrying laughter, pure and clear.

In the warmth of sunny days,
They rise and spin, a joyful dance,
Colors bright in playful ways,
Drawing hearts into their trance.

Children's giggles fill the breeze,
As they chase the fleeting spheres,
In these moments, souls find ease,
Bubbles pop, releasing cheers.

So let us dream, let us play,
With bubbles floating in the air,
In the magic of this day,
Together, we have not a care.

The Joy of Little Surprises

A note slipped under the door,
A smile hid in a glance,
Little surprises we adore,
Life's sweet, spontaneous dance.

Presents wrapped in simple bows,
Gifts that warm the heart's embrace,
In tiny joys, the magic grows,
Creating moments we won't erase.

From morning coffee's perfect brew,
To kind words whispered at night,
Life unfolds in shades anew,
Every surprise, a pure delight.

So treasure each small embrace,
In life's ebb and flow, you'll find,
The joy of love can't be replaced,
In little things, we're closely aligned.

Pathways Lined with Happiness

Down the lanes where laughter sings,
Sunshine dances on our feet,
Every step, a joy that clings,
On pathways where our hearts meet.

Trees sway gently in the breeze,
Flowers bloom in radiant hues,
Nature offers its sweet ease,
A canvas rich with vibrant views.

Hand in hand, we stroll along,
With every breath, the world is bright,
In this simple, joyful song,
We find strength in shared delight.

So let us wander, side by side,
Through every twist and turn of fate,
With happiness as our guide,
Together, we'll celebrate.

Canvas of Smiles and Sunshine

In the garden where laughter blooms,
Colors brush the air, dispel the glooms.
Each smile a petal, each joy a hue,
A canvas of warmth, created for you.

Sunshine dances on every face,
In this bright world, filled with grace.
With every laugh, the heart expands,
Embracing love with open hands.

The treasures found in moments shared,
A tapestry woven, hearts laid bare.
Each story told, a stroke of art,
In this canvas, we play our part.

As day declines and shadows play,
We hold these memories, come what may.
In every hue, our souls entwine,
A masterpiece of smiles, truly divine.

A Tapestry of Kindred Spirits

Threads of connection, tightly spun,
In the fabric of life, we are one.
Woven together, our stories blend,
In this tapestry, we find our mend.

With every whisper, a bond does grow,
Sharing our secrets, pain, and glow.
Hearts that know the other's song,
In this kinship, we all belong.

Moments stitched with threads of care,
A quilt of laughter, love we share.
In the quiet, or when we play,
We're kindred spirits, come what may.

As seasons change and time drifts on,
This tapestry holds where we have gone.
With every stitch, our spirits rise,
United forever, beneath the skies.

Sunbeams Dancing on Laughter

Golden rays spill on the ground,
In every giggle, joy is found.
Dancing shadows, a playful show,
Where laughter blooms, light tends to grow.

The breeze carries whispers of cheer,
In this moment, nothing to fear.
With every chuckle, spirits lift,
Wrapped in warmth, a precious gift.

Sunbeams flicker, a vibrant scene,
Painting the world in shades of green.
In friendship's arms, we find our place,
Laughter's embrace, a sweet embrace.

As day begins to gently fade,
These sunlit joys will not degrade.
In hearts that cherish every sound,
Sunbeams dance where love is found.

Tides of Contentment at Dusk

The ocean whispers secrets low,
As sunset paints the world aglow.
Waves embrace the shore with grace,
In this calm, we find our place.

Golden light spills onto the sea,
Reflecting all that's meant to be.
With every tide, contentment flows,
In tranquil moments, kindness grows.

As evening wraps the sky in dreams,
The world rests softly, or so it seems.
With hearts at ease, we close our eyes,
While stars adorn the twilight skies.

In the hush of dusk, we find our peace,
A simple joy that will not cease.
May these tides of calm forever last,
Creating memories from the past.

The Glow of Shared Secrets

In whispers soft, our hearts align,
With every glance, the stars entwine.
A hidden truth, we gladly share,
In twilight's glow, we shed our care.

The night envelops, shadows dance,
Entwined in dreams, we find romance.
Each secret held, like precious gold,
A story whispered, forever bold.

Beneath the moon, our thoughts take flight,
Through tales of love, we both ignite.
In every sigh, a promise made,
In shared moments, no fears invade.

As dawn unveils a brand new day,
Our quiet bonds will never fray.
In every turn, our spirits rise,
In the glow of truth, we find the skies.

Seasons of Leaps and Bounds

In spring we bloom, with petals bright,
Awakening dreams, in morning light.
Each leap we take, a dance so free,
In rhythms of life, come dance with me.

The summer sun, it warms our skin,
Adventures call us, let's begin.
We leap like children, hearts in flight,
Chasing the stars that fill the night.

As autumn leaves begin to fall,
We gather memories, one and all.
In every bound, we've learned to glide,
With hope in scenes, we won't subside.

Winter's chill may test our will,
But shared moments can deeply fill.
In seasons passed, we hold our ground,
Together still, in leaps and bounds.

Embracing the Ordinary

In the quiet morn, we sip our tea,
Finding joy in simple glee.
Each fleeting glance, a gentle bond,
In the mundane, our dreams respond.

The laughter shared over a meal,
In every moment, warmth we feel.
With open hearts, we greet the day,
Embracing life in our own way.

Through daily walks, hand in hand,
In every breath, we understand.
The routine's charm, a soothing balm,
In ordinary, we find the calm.

With every sunset's golden hue,
We cherish lives, both bright and true.
In simple joys, we weave our tale,
Embracing life as we set sail.

Mirage of Infinite Smiles

In a world that glimmers, bright and bold,
A mirage whispers stories untold.
Infinite smiles in fleeting sight,
Like treasures found in soft twilight.

We chase illusions on sandy shores,
Beneath the sun, where laughter soars.
In playful moments, joy ignites,
A tapestry of endless lights.

Through trials faced, we find our grace,
Beneath the surface, a warm embrace.
The mirage dances, changing hue,
In every smile, a shade of true.

Together, we build a canvas wide,
Painting our hopes with laughter beside.
In every glance, the magic swirls,
Infinite smiles adorn our worlds.

Dreams Adrift on Gentle Waves

On the sea where whispers play,
Soft reflections dance and sway.
Memories drift on silver tides,
Carrying hopes where light abides.

Stars above begin to gleam,
Guiding us through every dream.
With each wave, we learn to trust,
In the journey, rise we must.

Far horizons call us near,
With every swell, we lose our fear.
In the calm, our spirits soar,
Dreams adrift forevermore.

The Magic of Pure Exuberance

Laughter bursts like morning light,
Chasing shadows, taking flight.
With each moment, joy ignites,
Painting days in vivid sights.

Every heartbeat sings a song,
In this place where we belong.
Happiness in every glance,
Life's a wondrous, bright romance.

Take a leap, embrace the thrill,
In the magic, find your will.
With pure exuberance, we thrive,
Feeling truly, so alive!

Happiness in Each Step

Walk with me through fields of gold,
With every step, a story told.
A gentle breeze, a sunlit path,
In each moment, feel the laugh.

With every heartbeat, joy anew,
In every stride, let dreams come true.
Side by side, we chase the sun,
In this dance, our lives are spun.

Find the joy in what we share,
A tapestry beyond compare.
Happiness blooms in every pace,
In each step, we find our place.

A Canvas of Radiant Hues

Brushstrokes blend in vibrant cheer,
Colors whisper, drawing near.
Each shade tells a tale untold,
A story of the brave and bold.

Splashes of passion on the ground,
In every swirl, life is found.
From deep blue skies to fiery red,
A canvas speaks where dreams are led.

Emotions flow like rivers bright,
Creating worlds of pure delight.
In this art, we find our muse,
Life's a canvas, ours to use.

Treasures of the Everyday

In the morning light, we rise,
Birdsong dances, the sun replies.
Coffee brews, the world awakes,
Moments precious, love it makes.

A child's laughter fills the air,
Gentle breezes, no need to care.
Simple joys, a smile or two,
Treasures found in all we do.

In the garden, colors bloom,
Nature sings, dispelling gloom.
A walk, a chat, our hearts align,
In every moment, love will shine.

With gentle hands, we share our days,
Through fleeting time, in countless ways.
The treasures weave our lives anew,
In every heartbeat, me and you.

When the Stars Align

Underneath the velvet sky,
Stars awake, as dreams fly high.
Fates entwined, as hearts embrace,
Time stands still in this safe space.

Whispers soft, promises made,
In the night, our fears will fade.
Hope ignites with every glance,
When the stars align, we dance.

Guided by the moon's bright glow,
Paths converge and love will grow.
No more doubts, just pure delight,
When the stars align, it feels right.

Infinite possibilities await,
As we share this wondrous fate.
Hand in hand, we'll journey far,
In the magic, you are my star.

Carousel of Wonders

Round and round, the colors twirl,
Laughter echoes, joy unfurl.
Each moment spins in vibrant hues,
On this ride, we cannot lose.

Golden horses, wild and free,
Chasing dreams, just you and me.
Giggles rise, the world stands still,
In this magic, hearts we fill.

The music plays, a sweet refrain,
Memories made in sunshine rain.
With every turn, our spirits soar,
On this carousel, we crave more.

Embrace the whimsy, let it guide,
In this journey, we take pride.
Through every spin, love's light shines bright,
Together, we create our light.

In the Warmth of Togetherness

A cozy fire lights the room,
Laughter shared dispels the gloom.
In simple moments, hearts collide,
In the warmth, love won't hide.

Hands entwined, the world feels right,
Whispered secrets in the night.
Stories shared, both old and new,
In our podcast, me and you.

Comfort found in gentle grace,
Every smile, a soft embrace.
Through trials faced, we'll always stand,
In the warmth, together, hand in hand.

Seasons change, but here we stay,
Through the storms, we find our way.
In this haven, forever blessed,
Together, we've found our rest.

Trails of Merriment

Through sunlit woods we tread so bright,
Laughter echoes in pure delight.
Every step a joyful song,
In nature's embrace, we all belong.

With every path, a story tells,
Of whispered dreams and secret spells.
We dance along the winding way,
In trails of merriment, we play.

The rustling leaves, a gentle cheer,
Each moment shared, we hold so dear.
With hearts aglow and spirits free,
Together, just you, and me.

Beneath the sky, our laughter soars,
In the magic found within the shores.
We cherish trails where joy begins,
In every step, a life that wins.

The Euphoria of Simple Pleasures

A steaming cup upon the table,
Fragrant breeze, the heart is stable.
Sunshine filters through the trees,
In moments quiet, the spirit frees.

Gentle whispers of the night,
Stars that twinkle, pure delight.
Barefoot walks on grassy fields,
In simple joys, our heart reveals.

The precious smiles, the kind embrace,
In little things, we find our place.
With every laugh, the world feels right,
In euphoria, hearts take flight.

A stroll along the winding lake,
All worries fade, life feels awake.
In simple pleasures, we unite,
And find our joy in purest light.

Harvest of Tender Moments

In autumn's glow, we gather close,
With laughter shared, we cherish most.
Each memory sweet, a fragrant meal,
In the harvest of love, we feel.

With every story, bonds grow strong,
In tender moments, we all belong.
Hands held tight as seasons change,
The warmth of hearts, a sweet exchange.

We dance among the falling leaves,
Embrace the joy that love believes.
In every hug, we find our ground,
In simple treasures, life is found.

As sunlight fades, we share a glance,
In timeless love, we take our chance.
Harvesting joy, together we share,
In every moment, memories flare.

Adventures in Bliss

Across the hills, we roam so free,
In every step, a mystery.
With open hearts, we chase the sun,
In adventures together, we run.

Every journey holds a dream,
In laughter shared, we build a team.
With every twist, the path unfolds,
In stories rich, our lives retold.

Through valleys deep and rivers wide,
We find the joy in every stride.
In every view, a chance to see,
The beauty found in you and me.

As stars awaken, we sit and muse,
In blissful nights, we choose to lose.
In adventures vast, our spirits soar,
In each new dawn, we seek for more.

Chasing Dreams Under Open Skies

Under the vast and endless blue,
We chase the dreams that feel so true.
Stars above, they guide our quest,
In the night, we find our rest.

Echoes of laughter fill the air,
With every step, we show we care.
Beyond the hills, where shadows dance,
We seize the night, embrace the chance.

Winds carry whispers of our hopes,
In fields of gold, our spirit gropes.
Through valleys deep, we hear the call,
Together we rise, together we fall.

With every sunset, dreams ignite,
A future painted in colors bright.
Under open skies, we roam and soar,
Chasing dreams forevermore.

The Glow of Everyday Miracles.

In the morning light, a flower blooms,
Soft whispers of life in quiet rooms.
A smile shared, a stranger's glance,
Moments woven in a dance.

Raindrops glisten like tiny pearls,
Nature's magic in swirls and twirls.
A child's laughter, pure delight,
Sparks of joy that feel so right.

The warmth of sun on open skin,
The comfort found in where we've been.
Each heartbeat echoes tales of grace,
Every heartbeat finds its place.

In stillness, beauty calls our name,
In everyday, nothing's the same.
Miracles hide, waiting to shine,
Revealing love in every line.

Radiance of Each Dawn

As night retreats, the day awakes,
Golden rays on shimmering lakes.
The world adorned in softest light,
New beginnings chase away the night.

Birds sing sweetly, a morning song,
With each note, we feel we belong.
Blossoms open, greeting the day,
In nature's arms, we find our way.

Shadows fade, and hope ignites,
With dawn's embrace, our spirit lights.
In every breath, a promise lies,
The radiance of endless skies.

We gather dreams with open hearts,
As freshness fills, a brand-new start.
With every dawn, a story spun,
Radiance bright till day is done.

Whispering Laughter in the Breeze

Through the trees, a gentle sound,
Whispers of joy that swirl around.
Laughter floating on the air,
It teaches us how much to care.

Sunlight dapples where shadows play,
Children's giggles brighten the day.
In every corner, joy prevails,
In hidden paths, in vibrant trails.

With every breeze, stories unfold,
Of happy moments, pure and bold.
Nature sings, a playful tease,
With whispers of laughter in the breeze.

Together we stand, hand in hand,
Creating memories, oh so grand.
In every heart, the laughter we weave,
In the gentle breeze, we believe.

Sun-kissed Memories

Beneath the golden glow, we laughed,
Each moment rich, a treasure passed.
Soft breezes wrapped in sweet embrace,
Time stood still in that warm place.

Footprints trailing on the sand,
Echoes of a life so grand.
Sunset paints the sky with fire,
Filling hearts with sweet desire.

The warmth of days, forever bright,
In fading light, our dreams take flight.
Each memory a golden thread,
Woven deep, where love is fed.

We gather 'round the flickering flame,
Sharing stories, joy, and names.
In sun-kissed moments, we have found,
A treasure chest, forever bound.

Tides of Delight

Waves caress the sandy shore,
Whispers of the ocean's lore.
Sunlight dances on the sea,
Inviting all to come and be.

Shells and pebbles, nature's art,
Each a memory, a part.
Children laughing, running free,
Joyful moments, wild and free.

Seagulls soar on gentle winds,
Tales of adventure, where it begins.
The tides bring forth our laughter,
Creating echoes ever after.

As day gives way to twilight's hue,
We hold these tides, me and you.
In every wave, a dance of light,
Tides of delight, our hearts ignites.

The Fabric of Togetherness

Threads of laughter, woven tight,
In the fabric of our sight.
Fingers intertwined in trust,
A tapestry of love is just.

Moments stitched with care and grace,
Every smile, a warm embrace.
Through the storms and sunny skies,
Together we rise, together we fly.

With every challenge, hand in hand,
Igniting strength, a love so grand.
In this quilt of life, we stand,
Embracing all that fate has planned.

The colors blend, both bright and pale,
United we thrive, we will not fail.
The fabric of our bond so true,
A masterpiece made just for two.

Whispers of Joy

In quiet corners, laughter grows,
Little moments, how it flows.
Gentle whispers on the breeze,
Swaying softly through the trees.

Sunrise breaks with golden light,
Chasing shadows, casting bright.
Every heartbeat sings a tune,
Whispers dancing, night to noon.

Stars above, a glimmering glow,
In their light, our spirits flow.
Every smile, a shout of cheer,
Whispers wrap us, always near.

With every step, a joyful song,
In this dance, we all belong.
Gather 'round and raise your voice,
In the whispers of joy, rejoice.

The Dance of Sunbeams

Golden rays leap from trees,
A waltz across the green grass.
Shadows twirl in the gentle breeze,
Nature's rhythm, unsurpassed.

Flickers of light in the morning,
Kisses from the sky's embrace.
Each beam a song, softly forming,
A symphony of warmth and grace.

On the lake, a mirror bright,
Reflects the joyous sky.
Ripples dance in pure delight,
As sunbeams kiss the eye.

In twilight, hues of gold retire,
While stars wink from above.
The dance of light, a quiet fire,
Whispers secrets of love.

Heartbeats of Happiness

In laughter's echo, joy is found,
With every smile, a spark ignites.
Moments cherished, love surrounds,
In warmth of hearts, true light.

Through whispers shared, we bloom and grow,
Each heartbeat sings a tender song.
In every gaze, affection flows,
Together, we find where we belong.

With open arms, we face the day,
Together, we chase away the gray.
Hand in hand, come what may,
In the dance of dreams, we sway.

In quiet corners, joy persists,
In every hug, a wish grants.
Life's melody, a gentle twist,
In heartbeats, we find our dance.

Serenade of Smiles

A gentle grin, a sweet surprise,
Bringing warmth when days are cold.
In every laugh, a bright sunrise,
A tale of love silently told.

With playful glances, joy unfolds,
In simple acts, the heart finds grace.
In whispered secrets, happiness molds,
In every moment, we embrace.

Beneath the stars, we share our dreams,
A universe of hopes so vast.
In shared delight, the laughter beams,
A serenade meant to last.

When shadows loom and spirits dip,
A smile can brighten the darkest night.
In every heartbeat, love takes a trip,
A serenade that feels so right.

Embracing Every Color

In the garden, colors blend,
Petals kiss the morning dew.
In their hues, messages send,
A vibrant painting just for you.

The sunset paints the sky in fire,
Orange, pink, and violet gleam.
In every shade, our hearts aspire,
To dance within this brilliant dream.

Through every storm, a rainbow calls,
A promise following the rain.
In shadows deep, bright color sprawls,
Reminding us love's never in vain.

With open arms, we take it in,
Each tone, a note in life's sweet song.
Embrace the world, let the joy begin,
In every color, we belong.

The Color of Laughter

A splash of joy in the air,
Bright hues dancing everywhere,
Childlike giggles fill the street,
In every smile, life feels complete.

Rainbows arching in the sky,
Echoing laughter as they fly,
With every chuckle, spirits lift,
In this moment, life's great gift.

The world is painted in pure cheer,
Bringing loved ones ever near,
Colors blend, together play,
Laughter is the light of day.

In every joke and playful tease,
Hearts find comfort, souls at ease,
With laughter's warmth, we come alive,
In this bliss, our hopes will thrive.

Rising with the Sun

Golden rays peek through the trees,
Awakening the world with ease,
Morning dew, a glimmering sight,
Nature stirs, embracing light.

Birds are singing songs so sweet,
A symphony that feels complete,
Chasing shadows of the night,
God's palette painted bright.

With each sunrise, fresh hopes bloom,
Erasing all the lingering gloom,
Whispers of a brand new day,
Warmth invites us on our way.

Rising gently, dreams take flight,
Chasing worries, claiming light,
In the glow of dawn's embrace,
We find our strength, our rightful place.

Moonlit Chimes of Happiness

Underneath the silver glow,
Gentle breezes softly flow,
Whispers echo through the night,
Moonlit chimes bring pure delight.

Stars are twinkling in the skies,
Like a dance where laughter flies,
Every note a heart's sweet song,
Carrying joy, where we belong.

As shadows fold and dreams ignite,
Memory's warmth, a soft invite,
Together we sing, hearts embrace,
In this moment, time and space.

Moonlit chimes, our souls entwined,
In the magic, love we find,
With the night, our spirits rise,
Happiness sung in starlit skies.

The Essence of Delight

In the whispers of a breeze,
Joy is found among the trees,
Every bloom a vibrant song,
Life's essence, where we belong.

Laughing children, voices clear,
Moments cherished, holds us near,
Sunset paints the world in gold,
Stories new and memories old.

In warm embraces, hearts unite,
Finding peace in the soft light,
Every heartbeat, every sigh,
Spirals upward to the sky.

Delight is shared with every dream,
In the quiet, we can gleam,
With each joy, we celebrate,
In this essence, life is great.

A Tapestry of Delights

Gentle threads of laughter weave,
In colors bright, we dare believe.
Joy dances softly, hand in hand,
A tapestry of dreams so grand.

Whispers of secrets, cherished days,
In fleeting moments, hope still stays.
Stitches of memories, close and dear,
A canvas painted with love and cheer.

With every knot, a story spun,
Under the moon, beneath the sun.
Embroidered hearts in vibrant hues,
A masterpiece where love renews.

Echoes of Blissful Moments

Time stands still in fleeting grace,
A dance of joy, a warm embrace.
In laughter's sound, we find our song,
Echoes of moments where hearts belong.

With every smile, the world shines bright,
In gentle whispers, pure delight.
Memory's lanterns light the way,
Guiding us through each golden day.

Like ripples on a tranquil lake,
Each shared glance, a chance we take.
In the silence, our hearts align,
Echoes of bliss, ever divine.

The Sweetness of Simplicity

In quiet corners, candles glow,
Simple pleasures start to flow.
A cup of tea, a soft, warm chair,
Moments treasured, light as air.

Gentle whispers in the trees,
Nature's song on a soft breeze.
Embrace the calm, let worries cease,
In simplicity, we find our peace.

The laughter of a child at play,
Bright sunshine on a golden day.
Small things matter, love knows no bounds,
In simple joys, true happiness found.

Sunflowers in the Morning Light

Golden petals stretch and reach,
Embracing warmth, a radiant speech.
In fields aglow, they turn their gaze,
To greet the dawn in sunlit praise.

Dancing softly with the breeze,
A symphony among the trees.
Brightening paths where shadows lay,
Sunflowers bloom, chase gloom away.

With every dawn, new hopes ignite,
Their vibrant spirit shines so bright.
In morning's glow, we find delight,
Sunflowers whisper, "Hold on tight."

The Symphony of Everyday Wonders

In morning light, the world awakes,
With whispers soft, the day it makes.
A bird in flight, a leaf that sways,
These simple joys, the heart displays.

The rustling trees, a gentle breeze,
The flow of time, like a warm tease.
Each moment a note, a sweet refrain,
In life's grand song, we dance again.

The laughter shared, the smiles we give,
In every heartbeat, we learn to live.
Together we find, in quiet grace,
The symphony of our sacred space.

So hear the sounds, both near and far,
In every soul, shines a guiding star.
Embrace the wonder, let it unfold,
The beauty around us is worth more than gold.

Unraveled Joy in Simple Things

A cup of tea on a rainy day,
Warmth of the sun as clouds drift away.
An old book's scent, a gentle sigh,
In little moments, dreams can fly.

A child's laughter, a soft embrace,
The comfort found in a familiar place.
Barefoot on grass, the earth below,
The simple joys begin to flow.

Whispers of friendship, laughter shared,
In fleeting seconds, love is bared.
Each tiny spark, a radiant ring,
In our hearts, we find the spring.

So pause a while, take in the light,
Find beauty in the calm of night.
For in these moments, life doth sing,
Unraveled joy in simple things.

A Journey Through Golden Meadows

Where daisies bloom and soft winds sigh,
Beneath the vast and tender sky.
We wander paths where wildflowers grow,
In golden meadows, peace we know.

Each step we take, the heartbeat sounds,
Nature's beauty all around.
With every breeze, a story told,
In fields of dreams, our hearts unfold.

The sun sets low, a fiery glow,
Painting skies with amber flow.
A journey rich, both near and far,
In nature's arms, we find our star.

So come and roam through endless grass,
Let worries fade as moments pass.
In golden meadows, we are free,
A canvas bright, for you and me.

When Spirits Soar on Laughter's Wings

In joyous moments, spirits rise,
With laughter echoing through the skies.
A playful joke, a friend's warm grin,
In simple joys, we find our win.

The twinkle in an eye so bright,
Turns shadows into pure delight.
Together we dance, hearts aligned,
In every chuckle, love we find.

As clouds disperse, and sunlight streams,
We chase our hopes, we chase our dreams.
With open hearts, we lift our voice,
In laughter's realm, we all rejoice.

So let the giggles pave the way,
And chase the clouds of gloom away.
For when we laugh, our spirits sing,
A world transformed by laughter's wing.

Meadows of Freedom

In fields where wildflowers bloom,
The breeze sings a gentle tune,
Sunlight dances on the grass,
Whispering dreams as they pass.

Underneath the sky so vast,
Cherished moments, make them last,
Nature's palette, colors bright,
A sanctuary, pure delight.

Wandering paths, a heart set free,
With each step, find the harmony,
Every blade a story told,
In meadows rich with joys untold.

Revelations of the Heart

Beneath the stars, the silence speaks,
In hushed tones, the soul seeks,
The warmth of love, so deep and true,
Revealing secrets, old and new.

Moments shared, like fragile glass,
Reflections of the times that pass,
In each heartbeat, a soft refrain,
A melody born of joy and pain.

Open doors to worlds unseen,
Where shadows dance and hopes convene,
In whispers soft, the truth is found,
A symphony of love profound.

Singing Through Every Season

In spring's embrace, the flowers wake,
Joyful tunes the robins make,
Summer rays turn days to gold,
Stories of warmth yet to be told.

Autumn's chill with leaves that fall,
Nature's canvas, a vibrant call,
Winter's hush, a peaceful sigh,
Under blankets, the world sleeps nigh.

Through every change, a song remains,
In heartbeats that echo through the lanes,
A timeless rhythm, life's sweet grace,
Singing softly, the seasons' face.

Boundless Skies Above

Above the world, so high and free,
Clouds drift like whispers of a dream,
Sunset fires paint the horizon,
A canvas wide, our spirits risen.

Stars emerge in velvet night,
Guiding ships with their gentle light,
Mountains tall, and valleys deep,
Secrets unfurl in silence sleep.

Winds carry tales from afar,
Every breeze a wandering star,
In boundless skies, hearts take flight,
Dreams intertwine in the endless night.

Whispers of Sunlit Mornings

Golden rays touch the dew-drenched grass,
Birds sing sweet songs as moments pass.
A gentle warmth wraps around me tight,
In the embrace of a new day's light.

Flowers bloom with colors so bright,
Nature awakens, a beautiful sight.
Whispers of promise float in the air,
Hope dances lightly, free from all care.

The sky glows softly, a canvas divine,
Every sunrise invites us to shine.
With each heartbeat, serenity flows,
Reminding us gently of how love grows.

In whispered moments we find our place,
In the beauty of life, we embrace grace.
We walk hand in hand, no shadows nor fears,
In the sunlit mornings, joy reappears.

Harmony in the Gentle Breeze

The whispering wind through the trees does glide,
A symphony of nature, side by side.
Leaves rustle softly, a rhythmic dance,
Inviting every creature to take a chance.

Clouds drift lazily across the sky,
As melodies of nature softly sigh.
Each breath of air carries a tune,
The harmony grows beneath the moon.

In meadows lush, life awakens anew,
Colors blend softly, a vibrant hue.
With each gentle breeze, spirits lift high,
In unity, we find joy multiplied.

The world in motion, a tranquil embrace,
In the gentle breeze, we find our place.
Nature's orchestra plays a timeless song,
In this harmony, we all belong.

Laughter Beneath Starlit Skies

Under the blanket of night, we convene,
Stars twinkle softly, a mystical scene.
Laughter spills forth like sweet summer rain,
In the glow of the moon, we feel no pain.

Stories are shared, both old and new,
In the warmth of friendships, our spirits renew.
With every chuckle, the shadows retreat,
Beneath starlit skies, our hearts skip a beat.

The night wraps around like a cozy quilt,
Inside this circle, love is expertly built.
Each twinkle above reflects laughter's glow,
In the magic of night, we learn to let go.

Connected by joy in this vast universe,
We find our rhythm, an infinite verse.
Together we dance, our worries take flight,
In laughter beneath the starlit night.

The Dance of Colors in Bloom

In gardens where petals burst into view,
A tapestry weaves with every hue.
Nature's palette, vibrant and grand,
In the dance of colors, we all take a stand.

Crimson and gold, lavender, and teal,
Each stroke of beauty invokes how we feel.
Butterflies flit in this splendid affair,
As the flowers sway with the soft summer air.

The sun kisses blossoms, a warm embrace,
Creating a festival, a colorful space.
Each bloom a reminder of life's sweet refrain,
In harmony, joy dances within every vein.

Beneath a sky painted rosy and bright,
We find our truth in the colors of light.
In the dance of nature, our spirits entwine,
In the bloom's beautiful chorus, we forever shine.

The Bliss of Sun-Kissed Afternoons

Golden rays dance on skin,
Laughter rings in the air,
Children play without a care,
Nature's joy, a soothing hymn.

Gentle breezes softly sway,
Leaves rustle in delight,
Time drifts in fading light,
As the warmth begins to play.

A place where dreams can bloom,
Underneath the azure sky,
All the worries slip on by,
In this sunlit, sweetened room.

Moments cherished, joy in sight,
Held in hearts forever dear,
With the sun, we have no fear,
In the bliss of pure delight.

Cherished Memories in the Making

Fleeting glances, smiles exchanged,
New adventures start to grow,
Through the laughter, love will flow,
In our hearts, we feel unchained.

Every whisper, gentle tone,
Building bridges, side by side,
In each moment, hearts confide,
Creating bonds we call our own.

Snapshots taken, time preserved,
In the albums of our mind,
Every smile and laugh aligned,
Each embrace, a love reserved.

As we journey down this road,
With every step, we find our way,
Moments cherished every day,
Memories bloom, a precious load.

Whimsies of Heartfelt Whispers

Secrets shared beneath the stars,
Softly spoken dreams unfold,
In the night, our tales retold,
Binding hearts, no need for bars.

Tender sighs, a gentle breeze,
Dancing softly in the dark,
Love ignites a glowing spark,
In this world, we find our ease.

With each whisper, hope takes flight,
Kisses sweet as summer rain,
Joy and laughter, free from pain,
In our hearts, a shared delight.

Together, we will find our way,
Through whispers soft and true,
In the night, just us — me and you,
In this magic, we will stay.

The Euphoria of Spontaneous Adventures

Unplanned routes, the thrill awaits,
With laughter bold and spirits high,
We chase the sun across the sky,
Life unfolds, we celebrate.

Winding paths, surprises near,
In each moment, joy we seek,
Conversations, fun and cheek,
Memories made, free from fear.

From mountain tops to oceans deep,
Every journey, wild and free,
In this dance, just you and me,
In our hearts, new dreams to keep.

Spontaneity's sweet embrace,
Takes us where we long to go,
In the rhythm, love will flow,
Together, we have found our place.

Chasing Sunsets of Wonder

Beneath the sky all pink and gold,
We chase the light, our hearts unfold.
The whispers of the evening breeze,
Share secrets held by swaying trees.

The horizon glows, a fiery hue,
As day transforms, our dreams renew.
We wander paths where shadows play,
In twilight's glow, we lose our way.

With every step, the world ignites,
A canvas painted with our sights.
We grasp the fleeting moment's grace,
In sunsets' arms, we find our place.

Together bound, we'll always chase,
The fading light, the warm embrace.
So hand in hand, we run and soar,
For in this chase, we learn to soar.

Petals of Pure Bliss

In gardens lush where colors blend,
Soft petals whisper, they transcend.
Each bloom a story, sweetly told,
Of nature's love, both brave and bold.

The gentle rain brings life anew,
Awakening scents of earth and dew.
A butterfly flits from bud to bud,
In this pure realm, we feel the flood.

Sunlight dances through the leaves,
Enchanting hearts and filling dreams.
With every petal, joy ignites,
In fragrant air, our spirit lights.

So linger here, let time stand still,
In petals' grace, we find our thrill.
Together bound by nature's kiss,
In this sweet space, we find our bliss.

Heartstrings and Moonbeams

Under a sky of shimmering light,
We weave our dreams through starry nights.
Heartstrings tug where shadows gleam,
In the soft glow, we share our dream.

With every whisper, the world awakes,
In moonlit paths where love partakes.
The rhythm of us, a gentle song,
In countless moments, we belong.

As stardust twirls in cosmic dance,
We move together, lost in chance.
Through laughter shared and tears that flow,
In heartstrings' pull, our spirits grow.

With each heartbeat, our fate entwined,
Beneath the moon, our hopes aligned.
Together forever, we'll dare to dream,
In this embrace, we find our gleam.

Turning Moments into Memories

Each moment captured, fleeting bliss,
Beneath the stars, there lies a kiss.
In laughter shared and silent sighs,
We weave the threads as time flies by.

A smile exchanged, a warm embrace,
In every heartbeat, we find our place.
These simple joys, our treasures kept,
In quiet corners where secrets slept.

With every day, new tales begin,
In the dance of light, our souls will spin.
We write our story, page by page,
Turning moments into timeless stage.

As years unfold, we'll look back fond,
In sunset hues, of love so fond.
For every moment, wild and free,
Turns into memories, you and me.

Steps of Glee

With every step that we take,
The world shines bright, a joyful wake.
Laughter dances in the air,
Moments shared, beyond compare.

In sunlight's glow, we leap and spin,
Chasing dreams, where joy begins.
Footprints of laughter mark the ground,
In these steps, true bliss is found.

Nature sings, the flowers bloom,
Whispers of hope in every room.
Together we shine, lighting the way,
In the steps of glee, we choose to stay.

Through valleys low and mountains high,
We find our strength, we reach the sky.
With hearts aligned, we rise above,
In the rhythm of laughter, we find our love.

The Pulse of Connection

In silence shared, a heartbeat's call,
Two souls entwined, they rise and fall.
Words unspoken but clearly felt,
In this bond, true love is dealt.

Eyes collide, a spark ignites,
In that glance, the world ignites.
Through laughter's gift and sorrow's strife,
We feel the pulse, the dance of life.

Moments linger in tender grace,
A gentle touch, a warm embrace.
In every heartbeat, we grow strong,
In the pulse of connection, we belong.

Together we weave a tapestry,
Of dreams and hopes, a symphony.
In rhythm and rhyme, our lives entwined,
A bond so deep, forever defined.

Echoes in the Heart

Whispers of love in the night,
Echoing softly, a warm light.
Through shadows deep, they find a way,
To guide our dreams, to softly stay.

Memories linger, a gentle breeze,
Carried on whispers of the trees.
In the stillness, I feel the part,
Of every echo that fills the heart.

The laughter shared, the tears once shed,
Are notes in the song that love has bred.
In each heartbeat, the past resides,
In the echoes that love abides.

So let us cherish each moment clear,
The echoes of joy, the sounds we hear.
In the fabric of time, we're forever a part,
Woven together by echoes in the heart.

The Adventure of Now

In the midst of moments, we stand tall,
Embracing now, we heed the call.
With every breath, a chance to explore,
The thrill awaits, open the door.

With faces bright, we chase the sun,
In this adventure, we are all one.
Time stretches wide, possibilities bloom,
In the adventure of now, we find our room.

Hands intertwined, we leap and dance,
Every heartbeat, a daring chance.
In the laughter, in the sights we see,
We create our story, wild and free.

Let's seize the day, in unity stand,
With hope in our hearts, together we'll land.
In this great adventure, let's vow to be,
The authors of now, our spirits the key.

A Canvas of Bright Dreams

Brushstrokes of color dance in the light,
Imagine the wonders that take flight.
A tapestry woven with hopes anew,
In the heart of the night, we pursue.

Stars twinkle gently, guiding our way,
Every shadow fades, as dawn breaks the day.
With each stroke, a story begins to unfold,
A canvas of dreams, both brave and bold.

Whispers of magic fill the vast sky,
With every heartbeat, watch spirits fly.
In this realm, our souls intertwine,
Creating a world that's yours and mine.

Every color sings, a melody sweet,
In this vibrant place, our passions meet.
Together we'll paint, as life's brush sways,
On this canvas of bright dreams, we'll stay.

Serendipity's Embrace

A chance encounter beneath the old tree,
In unexpected moments, we find glee.
Fate weaves its wonders, a delicate thread,
With every smile shared, our spirits are fed.

Wander this path where the wildflowers grow,
Discover the magic in the ebb and flow.
Each twist and turn, a story unfolds,
In serendipity's arms, the heart boldly holds.

Unexpected laughter fills the warm air,
In the dance of the stars, we forget our care.
Together we wander, hand in hand,
In this beautiful chaos, forever we stand.

Grateful for moments that life redefines,
In the stillness, where serendipity shines.
Embrace each surprise, let the journey unfold,
In the tapestry of life, let the heart be bold.

The Sparkle of Morning Dew

Morning breaks softly with whispers of light,
Each droplet of dew a diamond in flight.
Glittering petals, the flowers awake,
In nature's embrace, the heart starts to shake.

The world is a canvas, painted anew,
With colors of dawn, a brilliant hue.
As sunlight cascades, shadows retreat,
In the sparkle of morning, the day feels complete.

Birds sing their praises, a melodic cheer,
As the dew on the grass brings the promise near.
Embrace the fresh start, let worries go,
In the warmth of the morning, let your spirit flow.

Every glistening drop tells a tale of hope,
In the early hours, we learn how to cope.
Life's gentle rhythm, a peaceful view,
Awaits in the magic, the sparkle of dew.

Echoes of Laughter in the Air

In the twilight glow, friendships arise,
With echoes of laughter beneath open skies.
Moments of joy, like fireflies gleam,
Together we weave a magical dream.

Under the stars, stories take flight,
With every shared smile, the world feels right.
In the hush of the evening, sweet voices blend,
Creating a harmony that knows no end.

Waves of nostalgia wash over the shore,
Each memory cherished forevermore.
Life's fleeting treasures, we hold them dear,
Echoes of laughter, a melody clear.

So let us gather, in this gentle embrace,
With love as our guide, we'll find our place.
In every heartbeat, in every prayer,
We dance in the joy of laughter in the air.

Milton Keynes UK
Ingram Content Group UK Ltd.
UKHW020936041024
449263UK00011B/564

9 789916 881477